N.Y.) Civil Service Reform Association (New York

Report of the Executive Committee of the New York Civil-Service Reform Association

N.Y.) Civil Service Reform Association (New York

Report of the Executive Committee of the New York Civil-Service Reform Association

ISBN/EAN: 9783741140907

Manufactured in Europe, USA, Canada, Australia, Japa

Cover: Foto ©Suzi / pixelio.de

Manufactured and distributed by brebook publishing software (www.brebook.com)

N.Y.) Civil Service Reform Association (New York

Report of the Executive Committee of the New York Civil-Service Reform Association

REPORT

OF THE

Executive Committee

OF THE

New York
Civil Service Reform Association

.READ AT THE ANNUAL MEETING, MAY 10, 1899

WITH APPENDICES.

NEW YORK
PUBLISHED FOR THE
CIVIL-SERVICE REFORM ASSOCIATION
1899

CONTENTS.

ANNUAL REPORT

OF THE

Executive Committee of the Civil Service Reform Association.

THE results of a year's work for civil service reform, in New York City and State, are in the highest degree encouraging to the friends of good government. The more serious losses of the previous year have been repaired. The so-called "Black act,"—one of the most vicious and dishonest measures of legislation of recent years—has been repealed, and its operation in the State Departments discontinued. The thoroughly unsatisfactory rules put in effect in the city, under the new charter, have been set aside by the Courts. A new law, general in its application, and superior to any civil service statute heretofore secured in America, has been enacted. The Governor, moved by sincere sympathy with the purposes of civil service reform, and aided by a practical acquaintance with its methods, is taking an active personal part in the work of reconstruction now made possible, and the prospect for further important advances is excellent.

The city rules, under the new law, must conform to carefully prescribed standards, and can have no effect until approved by the State Commission. As to the latter requirement the act confirms and renders more emphatic the decisions of the Courts. In correcting the shameful conditions that have developed under the present administration of city affairs and in guarding against their recurrence, it has a complementary effect hardly less important. Pending the revision of the city rules, no appointments of any sort will be recognized as valid unless made from competitive lists. Steps have been taken, moreover, to secure the annulment of a large number of appointments previously made, through evasion or open violation of the law, and the details concerning these will in due time be made public. The subjection of the city system to the State authorities, although necessarily limited, should serve to guarantee proper administration and fair results, in the future.

As a consequence of the practices made possible by the former rules, there have been excesses in the way of unnecessary and arbitrary appointments, promotions and increases of salary, that have cost the taxpayers of the city a sum which as yet can hardly be estimated. The importance of the new legislations from this point of view, is likely to be made plain in the course of the public discussion of the subject that seems imminent. So striking an example of the practical value of strict civil service rules would, in itself, be one of the most fortunate issues of the year's agitation.

The Civil Service Reform Association has been engaged actively and constantly in the matters referred to, and it has assisted as well, in the important work of the National League. Every effort has been made during the year to secure the correction of unsatisfactory conditions in the Federal Service, aided by expressions of public opinion against the proposed reduction of the classified service by Executive order. No order of this character has as yet been issued. It must be said, however, that while advances have been made in the State, there has been a general backward tendency at Washington, the effects of which threaten to become very serious.

It has been the custom, in presenting the annual report, to review briefly the progress of the reform, and the relation in greater detail of those matters with which the Association has had particularly to do.

THE FEDERAL SERVICE.

The attitude of the last Congress toward civil service reform was not favorable. The several amendatory bills introduced at the earlier sessions, and intended to modify the law, or to limit the area of its operation, were defeated, not because of a lack of sympathy with their purposes in either House, but principally for the reason that public opinion was unmistakably opposed to them. It had become plain, moreover, during the discussion of the subject, that the President possessed the power to fix 'the limits of classification, under the authority granted by the original act, and that the abridgment of that power by the vote of members of his own party might not be a courteous or a politic thing to do. The law was, therefore, left undisturbed, and the enemies of civil service reform in Congress derived such satisfaction as they could from the exclusion from the merit system of each new class of employees created.

The responsibility for maintaining the system as it stood at the change of administration, and for " extending it where-ever practicable," was thus left wholly to the President. More than a year before, President McKinley had announced that he would, if in his judgment the public interests seemed to require, remove a limited number of positions from the competitive class. When it became apparent that Congress would not act, the spoils seeking contingent caught desper-ately at this straw and requests for the inclusion of particular positions or classes of positions in the proposed list of "ex-ceptions " were received in great numbers.

In October last it was stated that , the number to be affected had been kept down to 2,500 and that an excepting order would be issued shortly after the election. Memorials were addressed to the President by the League and by many local bodies, including this association, pointing out that the offices in question, the list of which was unofficially made public, were, almost without exception, of a class for which non-partisan appointments, for reasons of fitness only, were peculiarly desirable. It was shown, also, that the reasons ad-vanced for restoring these offices to the patronage basis were not supported by the evidence of actual experience. Though the order has not yet been issued, it is still said that it will be issued, and that the delay is due to continued discussion as to the number and character of the positions it is to cover.

It is a matter of, perhaps, more serious consequence, that, pending the settlement of the proposed action, appointments and removals have been made in practically all of the classes under consideration in violation of the law, and that these offenses remain uncorrected. It has even been said, with some appearance of plausibility, , that the failure of the ex-cepting order to appear is due in large part to the fact that, since the simpler method of open disregard for the law has been adopted, the pressure for that order has greatly relaxed.

In the Department of Justice, the Internal Revenue Ser-vice, the field branches of the Interior Department, and in many Custom Houses the law has been treated as though it had no existence. When the Civil Service Commission, through the President, asked the Attorney-General for an opinion as to the validity of appointments without examination in his own department, a reply was received that as the positions in question would shortly be excepted anyway, discussion of the subject was more or less academic, and an opinion unnecessary. In practically every department of the Government, moreover, the provisions of the rules have been evaded, by various means, and many pages of the reports of the Civil Service Commission have been filled with the printed records of the unavailing protests made. The Executive rule of July 27, 1897, with relation to removals, has been disregarded, perhaps, more generally than any other, the evidence in such cases being particularly voluminous.

The Comptroller of the Treasury, Mr. Tracewell, of North Carolina, when asked by the Commission to co-operate with it by declining to pay the salaries of persons appointed without the required examination, declared, in reply, that the civil service rules do not have the force of law, that they are the creation of the Executive and that they are enforcable by Executive intervention only. Mr. Tracewell's " opinion " was written in a vein of coarse facetiousness. It was little short of insulting to the President, and as a construction of the law has been pronounced absurd. It stands for the present, however, as the rule of the Treasury Department. All persons whose appointments are certified by department heads, whether passed by the Civil Service Commission or not, will be recognized as legally entitled to compensation until the President, or the department officer himself, in each case, directs their removal.

In the Appraiser's Department, in the New York Customs District, the violations and evasions have been so numerous and so flagrant, that a joint investigation by officers of the Commission and the Treasury Department was held. The charges were sustained in ten specific instances, and in the case of some of these, indeed, corrections were ordered. The Appraiser himself, whose deliberate defiance of the law was clearly shown, has not been disturbed. It is commonly reported that in other branches of the Customs Service at this port, and in the Immigration Bureau as well, the intrusion of " politics " is more marked than at any time in a decade past.

It is not attempted to give, within the limits of this report, the facts in detail on which the foregoing statements are based. A special Committee of the National League has been appointed for this purpose and their findings, no doubt, will be published in full. Nor is the subject presented with any purpose in view other than to reveal the need of strict measures of reform within the service. The precedents established in many of these cases are apt to prove demoralizing. In some bureaus and offices they may be said to have already produced such an effect, and the evil seems to be growing. Although the subject has been brought to the attention of the President, from time to time, in the communications of the League, it seems unlikely that he appreciates fully the gravity of the present situation.

The tendency toward laxity at Washington has been greatly aided by the action of Congress in exempting from examination the clerks and others appointed in the War and Treasury Departments, for emergency purposes, during the war with Spain, and in organizing the Census bureau on the spoils basis. Seven hundred clerks were appointed under the war acts for periods averaging a year. The Civil Service Commission was prepared to furnish all of these, but the facts were misrepresented during the debate in the House, and the appointments were treated as patronage. The Census bill was passed with a provision permitting the Director to appoint three thousand clerks and statisticians after non-competitive examination only. This was precisely the plan under which the Census of 1890 proved such a costly failure. The outgoing Director, Mr. Carroll D. Wright, testified before a Committee of the Senate that if the Bureau were organized on the competitive, non-partisan plan, a saving of at least two million dollars would be effected. Memorials were sent from all parts of the country, mainly from scientific and business bodies, urging that this should be done. But the bill was passed in the form that the spoilsmen wished. Appointments are now being parcelled out to Congressmen and local party organizations. The examinations employed can at most serve only to bar out the absolutely unfit. As a check on patronage dispensation they will amount to nothing. In declining to place the Census Bureau in the classified service, the majority in Congress conspicuously disregarded the pledge of the Republican party, to extend the application of the merit system " wherever practicable."

The Civil Service Reform Association in New York will assist the National League as actively as may be practicable, in the preparation of its forthcoming reports.

NEW YORK. STATE.

At the time that the last annual report was presented the state civil service act, passed at the instance of Governor Black, and known commonly as the " Black act," was in operation in all of the departments and institutions of the state. In New York city its application had been annulled by the adoption of the new charter, and in the other cities of the state it had been superseded by the act passed on the last day of the session of 1898. In several of the state offices at Albany, where the heads of departments desired nothing more than the selection of the best fitted employees, the embarrassment of operating under the law was avoided by entrusting the examinations for "fitness," as well as those for "merit," to the Civil Service Commission. More frequently, however, the law was exploited as far as possible, for the purposes for which it was intended. In the Department of Insurance it was used so effectively that Superintendent Payn was enabled to increase his force of subordinates twenty per cent. in a year, without accepting a single applicant who had passed the open examinations.

It therefore happened that, as a result of the confusing legislation of the past year or two, at least four systems of widely differing character had come into existence by the first of the present year. New York city had its charter rules— the operation of which will be treated separately—the State departments were conducted under two adaptations of the Black law, and in the smaller cities the plan of the original law of 1883 was followed.

In his first annual message, Governor Roosevelt directed the attention of the Legislature to this anomalous condition and strongly urged the passage of an act repealing the Black Law and establishing a uniform system, for the state and cities alike, subject to state control. Such an act was prepared with the co-operation of a special committee of the Association, consisting of Messrs. Richard Watson Gilder, James McKeen, Edward M. Shepard, Thomas R. Slicer, William G. Low,

Horace E. Deming, W. Bayard Cutting, Samuel H. Ordway, and the Secretary.

This act was presented for introduction in the Legislature, after consultation with the Governor and other state officers and with the representatives of the civil service reform movement in Buffalo and other cities. It was introduced in the Senate by Mr. White, of Syracuse, early in February. In form it was amendatory of the act of 1883, repealing all inconsistent legislation and adding many important features suggested by the experience of the past several years. After some discussion it was determined to recast the measure, adopting a form amounting to a codification of all previously existing statutes, and less strict in certain of its general provisions. In framing this, the draft originally prepared was taken as the basis, and many of its more important sections were preserved intact. The section relating to cities, the most important of all, was practically unchanged. Several new features were adopted, however, that in the judgment of the Association's Committee greatly weakened the bill and raised serious doubts as to the wisdom of its passage. A hearing was given by the Senate Judiciary Committee, at which our objections were presented and discussed, with the result that all of the amendments proposed were accepted, save one. The bill was then reported and passed by the Senate by a majority of two—one Republican member only, Mr. Ambler, of Columbia County, voting against it, and one Democrat, Mr. Douglas, of Albany, voting for it. In the Assembly it was passed with slight amendments, necessitating re-passage by the Senate. Mr. Coggeshall, of Oneida, failed to appear at this critical moment, but the necessary majority of one was secured through the continued support of Mr. Douglas. On the following day—the nineteenth of April—the act was signed by the Governor, and went into immediate effect.

SCOPE AND EFFECT OF THE NEW ACT.

As the passage of this law will necessitate the complete recasting of the civil service system in New York, on radically different lines, a brief statement of its principal features, in this report, seems important

Seventeen previous statutes, enacted within the period from 1883 to 1898—including the Black law—are repealed and superseded. The existing rules for the State are continued, but are to be replaced by a new code, framed by the State Commission and approved by the Governor, before the 19th of May. Existing "merit" lists, meanwhile, are continued as eligible lists, and appointments, where necessary, may be made from them without further examination until new lists are prepared. The Commission is continued as at present constituted, with the same tenure, power and duties.

The State Service is divided into two branches, to be known respectively as the "unclassified" service and the "classified."

Ths former is to include all elective officers, heads of departments, legislative employees, and principals and teachers in the public schools. The latter will include all other offices and positions of every description.

In the classified service there aıe to be three schedules—thc exempt, the non-competitive, and the competitive. The excepted list will include only deputies and secretaries, where authorized by law, unskilled laborers, and "other subordinate places for the filling of which competitive or non-competitive examinations may be found to be not practicable." There are limitations placed on this grant of discretion in other parts of the act that make it certain that the excepted list will be far less in proportion than it now stands. Non-competitive tests will be employed for the grades just above that of laborer. The great bulk of the service is to be included in the open competitive class.

The methods of competitive examination in the State service proper will be substantially similar to those employed prior to the passage of the Black act, though in many particulars much more strict. The more important changes include the following :

1. The appointing officer is required to select the person standing highest on the appropriate eligible list, instead of choosing from among three, as heretofore. The appointee, if unsatisfactory, may be dismissed at any time during a prescribed probationary term.

2. Appointments to positions the duties of which are confined to a locality outside of Albany are to be made, so far as practicable, from among residents of the judicial district including such locality.

3. Appointments to positions in the exempt class are to be limited to one under each title, unless otherwise specifically provided. Subordinates who handle money are no longer to be exempted on that ground, the law permitting the appointing officer in such cases to exact an adequate bond, as a condition additional to the passage of an examination.

4. Persons appointed temporarily, in the absence of an eligible list, must pass a non-competitive examination, and cannot hold their positions for a longer period than sixty days.

5. Positions in the higher grades are to be filled, wherever practicable, by promotions, based upon merit and competition and upon the superior qualifications of the person promoted as shown by his previous service.

6. The provisions of the act of 1883 that no removal within the scope of the rules adopted "shall be in any manner affected or influenced by political opinions or affiliations" is continued, but the enforcement of this is left to the rules, which, according to the terms of the act, are to have "the full force of law."

The omission of the provision contained in the Act of 1898, for the filing in writing of the actual reasons for removals from all competitive positions, and for the granting of an opportunity to the person removed to make an explanation, is a loss that is to be taken into account in any complete estimate of the law. This omission the committee of the Association opposed strenuously, but the amendment, the effect of which would have been the continuance of the former plan, was rejected by the Senate Judiciary Committee. The Governor has promulgated a rule governing removals in the state service proper and this, it is hoped, will continue under the new act, to have the effect of law.

The State Commission, after recasting its own system, is to prescribe and enforce rules for the larger counties as rapidly as may prove practicable. The entire force of the county offices in New York and Kings, for instance—including those of the Register, County Clerk, Sheriff, District Attorney, Surrogate, and Coroners—will be classified, and appointments in each of them will hereafter be subject to the supervision of the Albany authorities.

The commission is also to have greatly increased powers in its supervision of all municipal commissions, and may compel compliance with its own standards of classification and examination. The initiative is not taken from the local bodies in any case where these standards are properly recognized, and it cannot be said, therefore, that there is any undue interference with correct principle of home rule.

Where a Mayor fails to appoint Commissioners the State Board may appoint them, and where the Commissioners fail within sixty days following their appointment to establish rules as required, the State Board may perform that function also.

They may by unanimous vote, and with the wrttten approval of the Governor, remove any municipal Commissioner for cause and after a hearing, and they may, by like unanimous vote, alter or amend any rule that does not conform to the provisions of the general law.

Finally, the State Board is directed to investigate from time to time the operations of local boards, and the acts of public officers generally with respect to the execution of the act. For the purposes of such investigations it is given all of the powers of a legislative committee.

The system in the cities is required to be as nearly as possible uniform with that in the State. In the smaller cities the important changes will be practically identical with those mentioned in the case of the State service. In New York the effect will be sweeping.

It may be added that two new methods of enforcement are provided that are apt to be very effective. The inhibition upon payments of salaries by fiscal officers, except at their personal risk, to persons appointed improperly, is reinforced by a provision to the effect that the appointee in such cases must be paid the full amount of the compensation agreed on, or in case there is no agreement, the actual value of his services, by the officer who appoints him. A right of action in such a case is granted against the officer personally. It is further provided that any taxpayer may secure a judicial review of a state or city classification containing exceptions from competitive examination that do not accord with the statutory or constitutional provisions, thus overcoming the apparently insuperable difficulties encountered by the Association in its efforts to establish this rule in the case of Chittenden v. Wurster.

It is not claimed that the new law is a perfect measure. It leaves a number of important advances still to be made, especially with respect to the fixing of moderate but more substantial safeguards against the unwarranted removal of competent and faithful employees. It is, however, as we have said, far superior to the statutes that it replaced, and its passage is to be counted as one of the distinctly valuable achievements of the present State administration. To Governor Roosevelt personally the highest credit is due. His effort was to secure the best obtainable. To this end all of his influence was lent, and his success in this respect has been the good fortune of the State.

The Civil Service Commission was partly reorganized in January by the appointment of W. Miller Collier of Auburn, as Commissioner, to succeed George P. Lord. Mr. Collier has shown an active and intelligent interest in the Commission's work, and bids fair to make a highly creditable record. With the co-operation of the Governor the Commission has already made important progress in the improvement of the examination system. The revision of the rules and classification it is understood, has been practically completed and will be made public within the time the new law prescribes.

The progress of general legislation during the late session of the Legislature was carefully observed by the Association's agent at Albany. A number of bills, designed to weaken the system, were opposed, and it is gratifying to note that none of these have become laws.

NEW YORK CITY.

To appreciate properly the situation in New York City it is necessary to consider the state of affairs existing a year ago and the progress of events since that time.

It was claimed by the Corporation Counsel on behalf of the City, that the Act of March 31, 1898, subjecting all city rules to the approval of the State Board, and regulating methods of removal, did not apply to New York. It was contended that the charter established an independent system, secure from change by means of any general statute. In pursuance of opinions given by Mr. Whalen to this effect, the rules approved by Mayor Van Wyck on March 5th, were continued in effect, and persons appointed under their provisions were paid their salaries from the City Treasury. During the year 1898 approximately 9,000 persons were appointed to positions in the city service. Of these, not more than 500 had passed examinations of any sort. More than half of the few who had been examined were taken from lists formed as the result of examinations held prior to the consolidation. Scarcely 200 had been selected from lists formed by the new Commission.

The rules permitted appointments without examination in the following ways:

(1) Through the extension of the excepted or "confidential" list practically without limit.

(2) By allowing temporary appointments, in the absence of eligible lists, for indefinite periods.

(3) By destroying the competitive feature of the labor registration system and allowing the appointment of laborers, without regard to the character of the services to be performed or the amount of compensation to be paid.

During the year in question 900 persons were appointed in the excepted class, as against 75 under Mayor Strong, 1,650 were appointed under "temporary" certificates, and 6,500 were appointed as "laborers." The number of competitive appointments, as has been pointed out, was insignificant. It is the common understanding that the great majority of the new clerks and others who are not serving after the lapse of a year or more as temporary men, are on the labor pay rolls. There has been nothing to prevent this. It is plain, moreover, in view of the actual number of competitive appointments, that the great bulk of the new places could have been filled in no other way. The average proportion may be seen from the following statement of appointments during 1898, in some of the larger departments.

	EXCEPTED.	TEMPORARY.	COMPETITIVE.
Executive,	20	25	0
Legislative,	15	13	0
Finance,	127	29	7
Law,	54	8	2
Health,	15	556	13*
Parks,	13	140	8
Docks & Ferries,	5	20	11
Public Imp'ts,	4	4	11
Sewers,	32	29	3
Water Supply,	29	35	3
Bridges,	12	32	0
Highways,	21	55	3
Public Bldgs. L. &. S.,	17	117	26
Buildings,	31	28	33
Charities,	35	136	45
Correction,	9	46	6
Municipal Courts,	22	56	0
Magistrates "	25	26	2
Borough Presid'ts,	10	7	1
Com'sion's of Accts.	68	0	1

*Exclusive of Temporary Physicians.

The Departments of Police and Fire are not included in

this list for the the reason that such appointments that have been made in these have been from the old lists.

The records of the appointments of laborers do not give the total figures by departments. These, therefore, are also omitted.

Although the letter of the Mayor's rules was violated possibly in but few cases, the provisions of law to which they were supposed to give effect, were virtually annulled. The result was that as new appointments could be made easily they were made frequently, and that the number of persons carried on the city pay-rolls was increased at a rate that has appreciably affected the tax rate. It followed, too, that the system of appointing at the dictation of "district leaders" and other local political potentates was re-established without difficulty. Although the law provides that there shall be no discrimination for political reasons in filling classified positions, heads of the city government have admitted that such discrimination is the rule. One such officer within the past few days has stated under oath, in the course of an examination in Court, that he has habitually violated the law in this respect. Removals were made for similar reasons and the provisions of the former act, requiring the statement of reasons in such cases were almost invariably ignored.

To secure the correction of these conditions the Association first appealed to the Courts. Several suits were brought to test the questions raised by the Corporation Counsel. These were undertaken by lawyers, members of the Association, who gave their services gratuitously. The question as to the validity of the city rules when placed in effect without the approval of the State Board, was brought forward in a number of cases, the principal of which, that of Fleming v. Dalton, was decided finally by the Court of Appeals in the Association's favor. The credit for this substantial victory is due very largely to Mr. Samuel H. Ordway, who served as counsel. It was held by the Court that the municipal rules must be submitted without delay to the State Board, but that, inasmuch as these rules had a legal effect on the date of their original promulgation, on March 5, 1898, appointments already made in pursuance of their terms should be recognized as valid. Removals made from competitive positions at any time since March 31 were declared irregular and void. Many reinstatements followed this decision, and the Municipal Commission, after a brief delay, finally sent their rules to Albany.

At a hearing given by the State Board the approval of the rules as they then existed was opposed by the Secretary of the Association, and a number of amendments were submitted as essential to a proper system. These were in the main adopted, and the City Commission, on March 21, was notified that unless the changes proposed were made approval could not be given. Before the local body had taken any further action the act of April 19 passed, and all proceedings under the old were practically discontinued.

The new law continued "all rules, regulations and classifications" consistent with its provisions that had received the approval of the State Board, but expressly repealed all that had not. It required among other things that not more than two-thirds of the Municipal Commissioners in each city should be members of the same political party, and that the Commissioners when appointed should promulgate new rules, with the approval of the State Board, within sixty days. Where no rules were left in force, as was the case in New York City alone, it practically prohibited all appointments until the new code might be placed in force. Mayor Van Wyck has appointed a new Commission, retaining Commissioners Knox and Dykman, democrats, and selecting Mr. Alexander T. Mason, republican, as the minority representative. The preparation of new rules is understood to be actively under way. Pending their promulgation the Commission will not audit the pay-roll of any person appointed to any office or position under the City government, except where the selection has been from the head of an existing eligible list.

The provisions of the law to which the rules must conform, that are changes from the charter rules, may be summarized as follows :

1. The excepted class will be materially reduced. Only one appointment will be permitted under each title so classified, and the reasons for each exception must be stated In writing in the annual reports of the commission.

2. The labor registration system, set aside by the present administration, is re-established. All applicants for positions in this class must be examined as to their capacity for labor and skill in the use of their tools, and appointments must be made from the registered lists in the order of original application. The employment of any person under the title of "laborer" to perform clerical or other work is made a misdemeanor.

3. Appointments in the competitive class are to be made in the order of standing, with proper provision for a probationary term, as in the State service.

4. Selections are to be made from the "most appropriate" list, instead of permitting a new examination, under any title the department officer may designate, for each appointment ; new lists will be formed only when it appears that the existing lists contain the names of none who are properly qualified.

5. Temporary appointments in the absence of proper lists may be made only after non-competitive examination, and then for a period not to exceed thirty days. Successive temporary appointments to the same position are forbidden.

6. The commission must advertise all examinations publicly, and is not permitted to dispense with advertisement in certain cases as at present.

7. Promotions are to be on the same competitive, merit basis as in the State service, and, "for the purposes of the act," all increases of salary are to be considered as promotions.

8. No person may be transferred to a classified position unless he shall previously passed an examination equivalent to that required for such position, or unless he shall have served with fidelity for at least three years in a similar position.

9. The Municipal Commission is required to keep a permanent roster of all persons in the classified service, giving the title and character of the office held, the date of commencement of service, the amount of salary, and other pertinent data.

10. Every city pay roll, before acceptance by the Comptroller, must bear the certificate of the commission to the effect that the persons named therein are enrolled on the roster as established, and that they have been appointed, employed, or promoted in full conformity with the law and rules.

The status of many of the persons appointed under the former rules may remain in doubt for a short time longer. A saving clause of the act provides, however, that no "liability, penalty or punishment incurred prior" to its passage shall be affected. Records were kept by the Association of all appointments, removals and other changes made during the year 1898, with the view of applying such judicial decisions as might be secured in the case of each. While many of these changes were practically confirmed as valid by the Courts, others, particularly those of the "temporary" class, were not. Similar records are being kept of current changes, and whereever action seems necessary in the future, to compel strict compliance with the law, such action will be taken.

The Association has been successful in a number of minor suits, one of which, that of Boyd v. the Commissioners of Accounts, involved a number of points of very considerable im-

portance. The Committee acknowledges gratefully the assist-
ance received in these matters from Mr. Ordway, Mr. Austen
G. Fox, Mr. Henry De Forest Baldwin, Mr. Everett Abbot,
Mr. George F. Canfield, Mr. E. P. Wheeler, Mr. F. W. Whit-
ridge and Mr. Edwin T. Rice, Jr.

Steps have also been taken to test the validity of the promotions made in the Police Department, without examination,
during the process of reorganization following the municipal
consolidation.

IN GENERAL.

It may be reported, in general, that the Association has
continued in correspondence, during the year, with the pro-
moters of local movements for civil service reform in various
cities and states, and that in many quarters substantial progress has been reported. Various meetings and hearings have
been organized, and relations have been maintained, where
desirable, with Executive officers and others in public positions. The offices at 54 William Street have been continued,
with the addition of an adjoining room, required for general
purposes, and the clerical force has remained unchanged. Information concerning the Association's work and the general
nature and purposes of civil service reform, has been prepared
and circulated, from time to time, in pamphlet form, and
through the newspapers. The Women's Auxiliary of the Association has continued to give efficient and helpful support
in these various matters. The publication of the official journal
of the League, "Good Government," has been resumed, and
this, in the future, will be mailed to each member under an
appropriation made by the Executive Committee for that purpose.

Since May 1, 1898, the Committee has passed favorably
upon one hundred and twenty applications for membership.

There is every evidence of a growth of public interest in
the work that is being done, and of a more general apprecia-
tion of its importance.

Respectfully submitted,

JACOB F. MILLER,
Chairman.

GEORGE McANENY,
Secretary.

New York, March 10, 1899.

TREASURER'S ANNUAL REPORT.

Balance as per report of April 30, 1898.................. $870.32

RECEIPTS:

Annual Dues............................	$2,245.00	
Sustaining Membership Dues..	1,125.00	
Life Membership Dues..................	200.00	
Subscriptions : General	1,923.50	
" Women's Auxiliary	1,000.00	
Returned Costs, Expenses of Litigation....	115.55	$6,609.05

$7,479.37

EXPENDITURES:

Proportion of Salary of Secretary..........	$3,300.00	
Clerk hire..............................	1,213.50	
Albany Representative	155.00	
Services of Accountant in connection with examination of city records	266.66	
Rent of Office.........................	450.00	
Printing...............................	380.26	
Postage Stamps and Stamped Envelopes....	287.00	
Subscriptions to *Good Government*	205.84	
Subscription to the National Civil Service Reform League	250.00	
Travelling Expenses....................	167.55	
Expenses of Litigation	235.93	
Telephone Service......................	111.50	
Office Supplies, Stationery, Furniture and Miscellaneous Expenses	291.64	7,314.88

Balance on hand May 1, 1899......................... $164.49

E. & O. E.

A. S. FRISSELL,
Treasurer.

ORGANIZATION

OF

THE CIVIL SERVICE REFORM ASSOCIATION

(OF NEW YORK.)

CONSTITUTION.

I.

The name of this organization shall be The Civil-Service Reform Association.

II.

The object of the Association shall be to establish a system of appointment, promotion, and removal in the Civil Service, founded upon the principle that public office is a public trust, admission to which should depend upon proven fitness. To this end the Association will demand that appointments to subordinate executive offices, with such exceptions as may be expedient, not inconsistent with the principle already mentioned, shall be made from persons whose fitness has been ascertained by competitive examinations open to all applicants properly qualified, and that removals shall be made for legitimate cause only, such as dishonesty, negligence, or inefficiency, but not for political opinion or refusal to render party service; and the Association will advocate all other appropriate measures for securing integrity, intelligence, efficiency, good order, and due discipline in the Civil Service.

III.

The Association will hold meetings, raise funds, publish and circulate appropriate information, correspond and cooperate with associations organized elsewhere for the objects set forth in this Constitution, and support all executive and legislative action which promote its purposes.

IV.

The conditions of membership shall be wholly independent of party preference. Questions shall not be discussed in the debates or in the publications of the Association upon party grounds. Neither the name nor influence of the Association shall be used on behalf of any party, or for procuring office or promotion for any person. But nothing in this article shall be construed to prevent the Association from opposing any candidate when in its opinion, or in that of three-fourths of the members of the Executive Committee, such course is demanded by the objects of the Association.

V.

There shall be a President, to be elected by the Association at the annual meeting, who shall perform the usual and prescribed duties of that office. He shall be, ex-officio, a member of all committees, with a casting vote only, and he may call special meetings of the Executive Committee whenever he thinks it necessary, and, with the assent of two members of the Executive Committee, special meetings of the Association.

There shall be ten Vice-Presidents, to be annually elected by the Association.

There shall be a Treasurer and Secretary, who shall perform the usual and prescribed duties of such officers. They shall be respectively appointed by the Executive Committee, and may be removed by them. The Treasurer shall be, ex-officio, a member of the Finance Committee of the Association.

There shall be an Executive Committee of twenty-five members, to be elected annually by the Association. Subject to these articles, the Executive Committee shall manage the affairs of the Association, direct and dispose of its funds, and from time to time make and modify by-laws for the Association and for its own action. The Executive Committee shall keep a record of its proceedings, and shall make a report to the Association at the annual meeting. No appropriation of money by the Executive Committee beyond the amount in the hands of the Treasurer at the time shall bind any member of the Association, excepting those members of the Executive Committee who shall vote for it. Vacancies in the Executive Committee may be filled by the President for the remainder of the term. Other vacancies may be filled by the Executive Committee.

All the officers of the Association and members of the several Standing Committees shall be, ex-officio, members of the Executive Committee.

VI.

Each officer of the Association shall continue to hold office until his successor has been selected and is ready to enter upon the duties of the office.

VII.

There shall be an annual meeting of the Association on the second Wednesday of May, at which officers shall be elected for the ensuing year, and other appropriate business may be transacted; except in the year 1898, when the annual meeting shall be held on the second Wednesday of January.

VIII.

Any person may be proposed in writing for membership by any member of the Association, and shall be admitted upon approval of the Executive Committee. Members failing to pay their dues may be dropped from the roll by the Executive Committee.

IX.

The annual dues of each member shall be $5, payable on the 1st of May, and each member shall receive the annual report and all other publications of the Association. Sustaining members, on payment of twenty-five dollars annually, and Life members, exempt from annual dues on payment of one hundred dollars, may be elected by the Executive Committee at any regular meeting thereof.

X.

All provisions of this Constitution, except those relating to the rights of members, and the term of officers, may be suspended or amended by a vote of two-thirds of the Executive Committee, subject to the approval of the Association by a two-thirds vote of the members present either at the annual meeting or at a special meeting duly called. Due notice shall be given before any such annual or special meeting that the approval of the Association will, thereat, be asked for such action of the Executive Committee, and the notice shall clearly state the effect of such suspension or amendment in the text of the Constitution. Any member of the Association may propose amendments to the Constitution, which may be approved under the same conditions.

BY-LAWS.

---

§ 1. The Annual meeting of the Association shall be held at such hour and place as the Executive Committee shall designate. The election of officers shall be by ballot, but any member not present may declare his vote by letter to the Secretary and it shall be counted.

§ 2. The meetings of each committee, unless otherwise especially provided for, shall be at half-past eight P. M., at which time the chairman shall direct the call of the names of its members and the Secretary shall record the names of those present and others as they appear.

§ 3. The order of business, before each committee shall be:

    1. The reading and correction of the records of the last meeting.

    And, thereafter, unless otherwise ordered, as follows:

    2. Any statement due from the Treasurer.
    3. Unfinished business from the last meeting.
    4. Report from the Secretary's office.
    5. Reports of standing committees.
    6. Reports of special committees.
    7. Proposals of new members and their election.
    8. Miscellaneous business.

§ 4. Regular meetings of the Executive Committee shall be held on the second Wednesday of every month except July and August, but if that day be a holiday, then on the third Wednesday. Ten members of the Executive Committee shall constitute a quorum.

§ 5. Neither in the meetings of the Association nor of any committee shall any member speak more than once on any motion nor more than ten minutes at one time, without unanimous consent, nor shall any person, or his actions, be characterized on party grounds.

§ 6. Special meetings of any committee may be called by its chairman or by any three members, and due notice thereof shall be given by the Secretary.

§ 7. All notices to a member shall be sent to his address filed with the Secretary.

§ 8. On the demand of one-fifth of the members present, at any meeting of the Association or of a committee, the ayęs and nays shall be called and recorded on any motion.

§ 9. All committees shall be appointed by the chair unless their selection shall be otherwise provided for.

§ 10. At each regular meeting of the Executive Committee, it shall be the duty of the Treasurer to make a statement of the amount of money in the treasury and of the place of its deposit, and at the annual meeting, he shall state the source of all moneys received and the use made of the same during the past year.

§ 11. The Secretary shall keep a record of the proceedings of the Association and of the Executive Committee, and perform the other duties assigned him.

§ 12. Without the consent of three-fourths of the members present, no vote which will declare or fill a vacancy or elect a member of the Association shall be deemed carried, at the same meeting in which it was first moved.

§ 13. It shall require a vote of two-thirds of the members of the Executive Committee present to pass any vote under which more than $100 will be appropriated or the Association be pledged for more than that amount, and the Executive Committee alone shall have authority to create any charge upon the funds of the Association. But neither said committee nor any officer or officers of the Association shall be authorized to create a personal liability against any members but themselves.

§ 14. There shall be the following Standing Committees to be hereafter annually selected by the Executive Committee:

(1) A Committee on Municipal Affairs, to consist of nine members, who, under the supervision of the Executive Committee, shall have charge of such part of the work of the Association as relates to the practical administration of the

civil service statutes and rules under the government of the City of New York.

(2) A Finance Committee of seven members, whose duty it shall be to devise and carry into effect, as the Executive Committee may order, suitable measures for raising funds, and to supervise and report upon the income and expenditures of the Association.

(3) A Law Committee of five members, whose duty it shall be to consider and recommend suitable legislation in aid of the purposes of the Association, and to promote such as may be approved; and whose duty it shall also be to represent the Association, under the direction of the Executive Committee, in any legal proceedings that may be necessary in order to maintain or to enforce the constitutional and statutory provisions affecting the state and the municipal civil service.

(4) A Publication Committee of five members, whose duty it shall be to prepare, select and recommend matters suitable for publication by the Association, and to take practical charge of the printing and distribution of whatever may be ordered printed.

(5) A Committee on Correspondence, of five members, whose duty it shall be to promote the organization of Civil Service Reform Associations, and to direct the correspondence with them; and whose duty it shall also be to conduct such correspondence with other organizations as in their judgment the advancement of the objects of the Association may require.

(6) A Commitee on Examinations, of five members, whose duty it shall be to consider and recommend suitable methods of examination for admission to the public service, and to consider the practical conduct of such examinations.

(7) An Auditing Committee of two members, whose duty it shall be to examine all vouchers and audit all accounts.

(8) A Committee on Membership to consist of five members, the duties of which shall be to use all proper efforts to increase the membership of the Association.

Each Standing Committee shall be competent to fix the number of its own quorum.

§ 15. These By-Laws may be amended, or new By-Laws added, by a four-fifths vote at any meeting of the Executive Committee; or by a two-thirds vote, provided a statement of the proposed change had been entered on the minutes at the last meeting.

§ 16. Amendments proposed under the last clause of the tenth section of the constitution shall be first submitted to the Executive Committee.

OFFICERS—1898′-99.

STANDING COMMITTEES.

MUNICIPAL AFFAIRS:

HORACE E. DEMING, *Chairman.*   GEORGE J. GREENFIELD.
C C. BURLINGHAM.   JOSEPH K. MURRAY.
ALFORD WARRINER COOLEY.   SAMUEL H. ORDWAY.
J. WARREN GREENE.   CHARLES W. WATSON.
ALFRED T. WHITE.

LAW:

EDWARD M. SHEPARD, *Chairman.*   SAMUEL H. ORDWAY.
DORMAN B. EATON.   EVERETT P. WHEELER.
J. WARREN GREENE.

FINANCE:

WILLIAM JAY SCHIEFFELIN, *Chairman.* JAMES LOEB.
DUNCAN D. CHAPLIN.   EDWARD D. PAGE.
J. G. PHELPS STOKES.

PUBLICATION:

ROBERT UNDERWOOD JOHNSON, *Ch'n.* GEORGE R. BISHOP.
NICHOLAS MURRAY BUTLER.   EDWARD CARY.
E. WALPOLE WARREN.

CORRESPONDENCE :

WILLIAM POTTS, *Chairman.*   WILLIAM A. PERRINE.
J. AUGUSTUS JOHNSON.   JAMES B. REYNOLDS.
CORNELIUS B. SMITH.

EXAMINATIONS:

SETH SPRAGUE TERRY, *Chairman.*   CHARLES COLLINS.
TRUMAN J. BACKUS.   J. H. C. NEVIUS,
NELSON S. SPENCER.

AUDITING:

HORACE WHITE, *Chairman.*   ETHAN ALLEN DOTY.

MEMBERSHIP:

EVERETT V. ABBOT, *Chairman.*   HERBERT SCHURZ.
J ACOB W. MACK.   CHAS. E. WOODBRIDGE.
RICHARD A. ZEREGA.

MEMBERSHIP ROLL.

(MAY 1, 1899.)

SUSTAINING MEMBERS.

AVERY, SAMUEL P.,	. 4 E. 38th Street, New York City
BOWKER, R. R., ...	. 59 Duane Street, New York City
BREWSTER, WILLIAM,	. Broadway and 47th Street, " " "
BROWN, WILLARD, . . .	Gallatin Bank Building, " " "
CARTER, JAMES C., . .	. 54 Wall Street, New York City
CARY, EDWARD, . .	. The "Times," " " "
CHAPLIN, DUNCAN D., .	. 64 Worth Street, " " "
CLYDE, WILLIAM P., .	. 5 Bowling Green, " " "
COLLINS, CHARLES, .	. 5 E. 16th Street, " " "
CRANE, RICHARD T., .	2541 Michigan Avenue, Chicago, Ill.
CRANFORD, JOHN P., .	. . Wakefield, New York City
CUTTING, R. FULTON, .	. 32 Nassau Street, " " "
DE COPPET, E. J., ...	. 30 Broad Street, New York City
DEERING, JAMES, .	Fullerton and Clybourne Avenues, Chicago, Ill.
DIMOCK, HENRY F., ...	. Pier 11, N. R., New York City
EATON, DORMAN B.. .	. 2 E. 29th Street, New York City
FRISSELL, A. S., . . .	. 530 Fifth Avenue, New York City
FULLER, PAUL . . .	. 100 Broadway, " " "
GILDER, RICHARD WATSON,	. 33 E. 17th Street, New York City
GODKIN, E. L., ...	. The "Evening Post," " " "
GOODWIN, J. J., ...	. 11 W. 54th Street, " " "
GRACE, WILLIAM R., . . .	3 Hanover Square, " " "
HEMENWAY, AUGUSTUS, .	. 10 Tremont Street, Boston, Mass.
JACOBI, A., ...	. 110 W. 34th Street, New York City
JOHNSON, ROBERT UNDERWOOD, .	33 E. 17th Street, " " "
KUNHARDT, WILLIAM B.,	. 1 Broadway, New York City
LOEB, SOLOMON,	P. O. Box 1193, New York City
MACK, JACOB W., . . .	. 92 Liberty Street, New York City
MACY, V. EVERIT, . . .	. 18 W. 53rd Street, " " "
MAITLAND, ALEXANDER, .	. 14 E. 55th Street, " " "
MASON, FRANCIS O., . .	. . . . . Geneva, N. Y.

MAXWELL, ROBERT. . . . . 62 Worth Street, New York City
MINTURN, ROBERT SHAW, . . Bowling Green Bldg., " " "
MORTON, LEVI P., ... 32 Nassau Street, " " "

ORDWAY, SAMUEL H., . . . 31 Nassau Street, " " "
OTTENDORFER, OSWALD, . . 3 Tryon Row, " " "

PAGE, EDWARD D., . . . 66 Leonard Street, New York City
PINCHOT, JAMES W., . . . 3 Gramercy Park, " " "
POWERS, NATHANIEL B., ... Lansingburg, N. Y.

RANDOLPH, STUART F., . . . 31 Nassau Street, New York City

SCHERMERHORN, W. C., . . . 49 W. 23rd Street, New York City
SCHIEFFELIN, WILLIAM JAY, . . 35 W. 57th Street, " " "
SCHIFF, JACOB H., ... P. O. BOX 1193 " " "
SCHWAB, GUSTAV H., ... 2 Bowling Green, " " "
SCRYMSER, JAMES A., ... 107 E. 21st Street, " " "
SMITH, CORNELIUS B., ... 101 E. 69th Street, " " "
SPENCER, NELSON S., ... 31 Nassau Street, " " "
SPEYER, JAMES, ... 257 Madison Avenue, " " "
STETSON, FRANCIS LYNDE, . . 15 Broad Street, " " "
STOKES, ANSON PHELPS, . . . 47 Cedar Street, " " "
STRAUS, OSCAR S., . . . American Legation, Constantinople

WARE, WILLIAM R., . . 41 E. 49th Street, New York City
WATSON, CHARLES W., . . 40 W. 59th Street, " " "
WHITE, ALFRED T., . . 130 Water Street, " " "
WUNDERLICH, F. W., . . . 165 Remsen Street, Brooklyn

Abbot, Everett V., ... 55 William Street, New York City
Abbott, Lyman, ... 287 Fourth Avenue, " " "
Achelis, John, ... 68 Leonard Street, " " "
Adams, Charles Frederick, . . . 100 Broadway, " " "
Adams, Joseph, ... Union Stock Yards, Chicago, Ill.
Adams, Thatcher M., ... 36 Wall Street, New York City
Adler, Felix, ... 1524 Park Avenue, " " "
Affeld, Francis O., ... 873 President Street, Brooklyn
Agar, John G., ... 31 Nassau Street. New York City
Agnew, Andrew Gifford, . . . 7 Nassau Street, " " "
Aiken, William A., . . . 65 Washington Street, Norwich, Conn.
Aitken, John W. . . . . . 873 Broadway, New York City
Allen, Elmer A., ... 80 Broadway, " " "
Allen, Franklin, ... 371 Fulton Street, Brooklyn
Alsop, Reese F., ... 79 Remsen Street, "
Anderson, Frank E., ... 715 Broadway, New York City

Babbitt, Henry A., ... Pomfret Centre, Conn.
Backus, Truman J., ... Packer Institute, Brooklyn

Bacon, Gorham, ... 63 W. 54th Street, New York City
Bagley, Valentine N., ... 641 Washington Street, New York City
Baker, Charles R., ... 244 Washington Street, Brooklyn
Baldwin, Henry de Forest, . . . 30 Broad Street, New York City
Ball, Thomas P., ... 312 St. James Place, Brooklyn
Bangs, L. Bolton, ... 31 E. 44th Street, New York City
Bannard, Otto T., ... 30 Broad Street, " " "
Bard, Albert Sprague, ... 30 Broad Street, " " "
Barker, Benjamin, ... 120 Broadway. " " "
Barney, A. H., (Life) . . . . 101 E. 38th Street, " " "
Barney, Danford N., ... Farmington, Conn.
Barrett, Frank R., ... Box 616, Portland, Me.
Batterman, Henry, ... 360 Clinton Avenue, Brooklyn
Baylies, Edmund L., ... 54 Wall Street, New York City
Beaman, Charles C., ... 52 Wall Street, " " "
Beebe, William H. H., . . Columbia University, " " "
Beekman, Gerard, ... 47 Cedar Street, " " "
Biggs, Charles, ... 13 Astor Place, " " "
Bishop, George R., ... 142 E. 18th Street, " " "
Bishop, Heber R., ... 15 Broad Street, " " "
Bishop, Joseph B., ... "The Evening Post" " " "
Bispham, William, ... 66 Broadway, " " "
Blagden, George, ... 51 Wall Street, " " "
Bode, Frederick H., ... care Gage Bros., Chicago, Ill.
Borden, M. C. D., ... Box 2894, New York City
Bowen, C. Winthrop, ... 3 E. 10th Street, " " "
Brewster, Charles O., ... 32 Liberty Street, " " "
Briesen, Arthur von, (Life) . . . 229 Broadway, " " "
Brigham, William T., ... Carnegie Apartments, " " "
Briscoe, S. William, ... 426 Central Park, W., " " "
Brookfield, William, ... 218 Broadway, " " "
Brown, Henry T., ... 192 Lincoln Place, Brooklyn
Brownell, T. Frank, ... 131 E. 15th Street, New York City
Brownell, William C., ... 153 Fifth Avenue, " " "
Bruce, James M., ... Yonkers, N. Y.
Brush, W. Franklin, ... 16 E. 37th Street, New York City
Buckingham, C. L., ... 195 Broadway, " " "
Bunnell, James S., . 85 New Montgomery Street, San Francisco, Cal.
Burlingham, Charles C., ... 45 William Street, New York City
Burt, Silas W., ... 30 Broad Street, " " "
Bush, J. Adriance, ... 100 Broadway. " " "
Butler, Nicholas Murray, . . . 119 E. 80th Street, " " "
Byrne, James, ... 30 Broad Street, " " "

Cadwalader, John L., . . . 36 Wall Street, New York City
Canfield, George F., ... 48 Wall Street, " " "
Carnegie, Andrew, (Life) . . . 5 West 51st Street, " " "
Carter, Frederick B., ... 61 Church Street, Montclair, N. J.

Carter, George F.,	. . . . Fanwood, N. J.
Cary, Clarence,	. . . . 59 Wall Street, New York City
Cassatt, George M.,	. . . 327 Broadway, " " "
Cauldwell, John B.,	. . . . . . Southampton, N. Y.
Chadwick, John White,	. . . . 626 Carlton Avenue, Brooklyn
Chamberlain, D. H.,	. . . . .40 Wall Street, New York City
Chamberlain, L. T.,	. . . . 222 W. 23 Street, " " "
Chambers, William,	. . . . 59 Liberty Street, " " "
Chandler, Frank R.,	. . . . 110 Dearborn Street, Chicago, Ill.
Chanute, Octave,	. . . 413 East Huron Street, " "
Chase, George,	. . . . . 35 Nassau Street, New York City
Chauncey, Daniel,	. . . . . 129 Joralemon Street, Brooklyn
Cheney, F. W.,	. . . . South Manchester, Conn.
Cheney, George L.,	. . . . . 131 E. 57th Street, New York City
Choate, Joseph H.,	. . . . . . American Embassy, London
Choate, William G.,	. . . . 40 Wall Street, New York City
Claflin, John,	. . . . . .224 Church Street, " " "
Claghorn, Charles,	. . Bedford Avenue, cor. Fulton Street, Brooklyn
Clarke, Samuel B.,	. . . . 100 Broadway, New York City
Cleveland, Treadwell,	. . . . 52 Wall Street, " " "
Cochran, Alexander,	. . . . 127 Seventh Avenue, Brooklyn
Collins, Stephen W.,	. . . . 69 Wall Street, New York City
Collyer, Robert,	. . . . 1672 Broadway, " " "
Conger, Clarence R.,	. . . .45 William Street, " " "
Conger, Henry C.,	. . . . 140 W. 82d Street, " " "
Cook, George J.,	. . . . 32 Howard Street, " " "
Cook, Charles D.,	. . . . . 162 Remsen Street, Brooklyn
Cooley, Alford Warriner,	. . . . . Westchester, New York City
Cope, F. Hazen,	. . . . Germantown, Pa.
Cope, Francis R.,	. . . 1 Walnut Street, Philadelphia
Cowen, Esek K.,	. . . 45 William Street, New York City
Cowing, John H.,	. . . . 186 Main Street, Buffalo
Cowperthwait, J. Howard,	. 195 Park Row, New York City
Crane, Frederick,	. . . . Bloomfield, N. J.
Cranford, Walter V.,	. . . 215 Montague Street, Brooklyn
Cravath, Paul D.,	. . . 120 Broadway, New York City
Creevey, John J.,	. . . 41 Wall Street, " " "
Cromwell, Frederic,	. . . 32 Nassau Street, " " "
Cromwell, James W.,	. . . 1 Greene Street, " " "
Cromwell, Lincoln,	. . . 1 Greene Street, " " "
Cross, R. T.,	. . . 32 Nassau Street, " " "
Curtis, William E.,	. . . 52 William Street, " " "
Cushing, William E.,	. Society for Savings Bldg., Cleveland, O.
Cutler, Arthur H.,	. 20 E. 50th Street, New York City
Cutting, W. Bayard,	. 24 E. 72nd Street, " " "
Daboll, Henry E.,	. . 30 Broad Street, New York City
Dahlgren, John Vinton,	20 W. 56th Street, " " "

Daly, Charles P., ... 84 Clinton Place, New York City
Damrosch, Frank, ... Carnegie Hall, " " "
Dana, Charles L., . . 50 W. 46th Street, " " "
Davidson, Charles A., ... 71 Wall Street, " " "
Davies, Julien T., . . . 32 Nassau Street, " " "
Davies, William Gilbert, . 32 Nassau Street, " " "
Davis, Benjamin P., . . 107 Wall Street, " " "
Day, Clarence S., . . 38 Wall Street, " " "
DeForest, R. W., . . 30 Broad Street, " " "
De Forest, Robert W., . . . 62 William Street, " " "
Delano, Warren, Jr., ... 1 Broadway, " " "
Delavan, D. Bryson, ... 1 E. 33d Street, " " "
Deming, Horace E., ... 18 William Street, " " "
Demuth, William, ... 524 Fifth Avenue, " " "
Dettmer, Jacob G., ... 27 Prospect Park W., Brooklyn
Devine, Edward T., ... 170 W. 81st Street, New York City
Dickinson, Robert L., ... 168 Clinton Street, Brooklyn
Dodge, William E., ... 11 Cliff Street, New York City
Doty, Ethan Allen, ... 726 St. Marks Place, Brooklyn
Dougherty, J. Hampden, ... 7 Nassau Street, New York City
Dow, Frederick G., ... 61 W. 17th Street, " " "
Dows, Tracy, ... Room 102, Produce Exchange, " " "
Du Bois, John C., ... 318 Allen Street, Hudson, N. Y.
Dunham, Edward K., ... 388 E. 26th Street, New York City
Dunham, James H., ... 340 Broadway, " " "
Dunham, Lawrence, ... 72 Bible House, " " "
Dunning, S. Wright, ... 80 Madison Avenue, " " "

Elderkin, John, . . . 150 W. 83d Street, New York City
Eliot, Charles W., ... Cambridge, Mass.
Elkins, Stephen B., . . 1626 K Street, Washington, D. C.
Ely, Alfred, ... 31 Nassau Street, New York City
Ely, Arthur H., ... 56 Wall Street, " " "
Emmons, Arthur B, ... 60 Park Avenue, " " "
Emmons, J. Frank, ... 56 Broadwa y, " " "
Emmons, Samuel F., . U. S. Geological Survey, Washington, D. C.
Ewart, Richard H., . . . 115 Franklin Street, New York City

Fairchild, Benjamin T., . . 70 W. 52d Street, New York City
Fairchild, Charles S., . 46 Wall Street, " " "
Faure, John P., . . 70 Franklin Street, " " "
Fisher, George H., . 308 Walnut Street, Philadelphia, Pa.
Fisher, George H., . . . 310 Throop Avenue, Brooklyn
Floyd, John G., . . 117 E. 25th Street, New York City
Foster, Abbott, . 240 W. 73rd Street, " " "
Fox, Austen G., (Life), . 45 W. 33d Street, " " "
Francis, David G., . . 7 W. 43d Street, " " "
Frankenheimer, John, . 22 Broad Street, " " "
Frissell, H. B., ... Hampton, Va.

Frothingham, Benjamin T., . . . 188 Columbia Heights, Brooklyn
Fuller, Frank, ... , . 61 Fifth Avenue, New York City
Fullerton, Alexander, (Life), . . 5 University Place, " " "
Galbreath, Thomas, ... Memphis, Tenn.
Garrison, Wendell P., ... 206 Broadway, New York City
Gibbs, Theodore K., ... 146 Broadway, " "
Gibbs, Wolcott, ... Newport, R. I.
Gibson, William J., ... 32 Nassau Street, New York City
Goadby, Clarence, ... 21 W. 35th Street, " " "
Goddard, George A., ... 10 Tremont Street, Boston, Mass.
Goldman, Julius, ... 11 Pine Street, New York City
Goldmark, James,. . . . . . 121 Worth Street, " " "
Goodale, John McGregor, ... 18 Wall Street, " " "
Goodnow, Frank J., ... 25 W. 94th Street, " " "
Gould, Elgin R. L., ... 281 Fourth Avenue, " " "
Graef, Edward L., ... 58 Court Street, Brooklyn
Grant, De Forest, ... 22 E. 49th Street, New York City
Green, George Walton, ...'11 Pine Street, " " "
Green, Noah, ... 10 E. 130th Street, " " "
Greene, Edward R., ... 15 Broad Street, " " "
Greene, Jacob L.. . . . . Hartford, Conn.
Greene, J. Warren, ... 3 Broad Street, New York City
Greenfield, George J., ... 32 Broadway, " " "
Griswold, J. N. A., ... 71 South Street, " " "
Guthrie, William D., ... 40 Wall Street, " " "
Gwynne, Arthur C., ... Rye, N. Y.
Gwynne, John A., ... " "

Hall, Elial F., ... Camden, Wilcox Co., Ala.
Hall, Valentine G., ... 1 Nassau Street, New York City
Hamilton, E. Luther, ... 146 Broadway, " " "
Hand, Augustus N., ... 30 Broad Street, " " "
Harbeck, Charles T., . . . 306 Lexington Avenue, " " "
Hardon, Henry Winthrop, . . . 313 W. 71st Street, " " "
Harriot, S. Carman, ... 454 W. 23d Street, " " "
Hart, John G., ... 975 Second Avenue, Brooklyn
Hartshorne, B. M., . . . 44 Exchange Place, New York City
Heath, Frank E., ... 94 Liberty Street, " " "
Healy, A. Augustus, ... 198 Columbia Heights, Brooklyn
Henderson, Harold G., . . . 128 E. 34th Street, New York City
Henriques, Charles A., . . . 48 Exchange Place, " " "
Hentz, Henry, ... 769 St. Marks Avenue, Brooklyn
Hentz, Leonard S., . . . 769 St Marks Avenue, "
Hepburn, H. J., ... 369 W. 23d Street, New York City
Heydecker, Edward L., . . . 111 Broadway, " " "
Hicks, Benjamin D., ... Old Westbury, N. Y.
Higginson, James J., . . . 7 Nassau Street, New York City
Hill, J. E. R., ... 115 High Street, Boston, Mass.
Hinrichs, Frederick W., . . . 115 Broadway, New York City

Hitchcock, Welcome G., (Life) . . 453 Broome Street, New York City
Hobart, Henry L., ... 120 Front Street, " " "
Hoe, Richard M., . . . Room 102, Produce Exchange, " " "
Holls, Frederick W., ... 120 Broadway, " " "
Holt, George C., ... 34 Pine Street, " " "
Holt, Henry, ... 29 W. 23d Street, " " "
Hooper, Franklin W., ... 71 St. James Place, Brooklyn
Hoppin, William W., ... 111 Broadway, New York City
Hornblower, William B., ... 30 Broad Street, " " "
Howland, Charles P., ... 35 Wall Street, " " "
Hubbard, Thomas H., ... 16 W. 58th Street, " ' "
Hubbell, Charles Bulkeley, ... 2 Wall Street, " " "
Hull, Charles A., ... 72 Wall Street, " " "
Huntington, William R., ... 804 Broadway, " " "

Iles, George, . . Park Avenue Hotel, New York City
Ireland, F. G., . . 142 E. 40th Street, " " "
Isaacs, Myer S., . . . 27 Pine Street, " " "

Jackson, Frederick W., ... Westchester, N. Y.
James, D. Willis, ... 11 Cliff Street, New York City
Jardine, John, ... 1262 Broadway, " " "
Jay, William, ... 48 Wall Street, " " "
Jefferson. Joseph, . . . , , . . Buzzards Bay, Mass.
Jennings, Frederick B., . . . 15 Broad Street, New York City
Jesup, Morris K., ... 44 Pine Street, " " "
Johnson, Eastman,. . . . 66 W. 55th Street, " " "
Johnson. J. Augustus, . . . 58 William Street, " " "
Johnson, James G., ... 655 Broadway, " " "
Jones, Edward H., . . Naval Office, Custom House, " " "
Justi, Herman, ... Nashville, Tenn.

Kelly, Edmond, . . 107 E. 60th Street, New York City
Kenneson, Thaddeus D., . . . 13 William Street, " " "
Kenyon, Alan D., ... 150 Nassau Street, " " "
Kenyon, William Houston. . . 150 Nassau Street, " " "
Keppler, Rudolph, . . . , . 39 Broad Street, " " "
Kernan, John D., ... 37 Liberty Street, " " "
Kidder, Camillus G., . . . 82 Nassau Street, " " "
Kimball, A. R., ... Orange, N. J.
Kinnicutt, Francis P., . . . 42 W. 37th Street, New York City
Kissell, Gustav E., (Life), . . 54 Wall Street, " " "
Klupfel, Charles, . . . 2 Bowling Green, " " "
Knauth, Antonio, . 233 West 70th Street, " " "
Knauth, Percival, . . 13 William Street, " " "
Kunhardt, Henry R., . . 124 W. 74th Street, " " "

Lambert, Henry, ... West Newton, Mass.
Lambert, William B., . Highland Avenue, Cambridge Mass.
Lansing J. Townsend, ... 82 State Street, Albany

Larocque, Joseph, ... P. O. Box 2911, New York City
Larremore, Wilbur, . . . 32 Nassau Street. " " "
Lawrence, Cyrus J., . . . 31 Broad Street, New York City
Lawrence, Richard H., . . . 31 Broad Street, " " "
Lea, Henry Charles, . . . 2000 Walnut Street, Philadelphia
Learned, James E., . . . 56 E. 54th Street, New York City
Leavens, George St. J., . . 72 Bible House, " " "
Leavitt, J. Brooks, ... 111 Broadway " " "
Ledoux, Albert R., ... 9 Cliff Street, " " "
Lee, W. H. L., ... 20 Nassau Street, " " "
Lent, Edward B., ... 200 Joralemon Street, Brooklyn
Lewis, August, ... 151 Greene Street, New York City
Lewis, Richard V., . . ' . . 120 W. 42d Street, " " "
Lockwood, Benoni, ... 56 Irving Place, " " "
Loeb, James, ... 27 Pine Steet, " " "
Logan, Walter S., ... 617 Fifth Avenue, " " "
Loines, Stephen, ... 26 Garden Place, Brooklyn
Lord, Franklin B., ... 120 Broadway, New York City
Lovell, Joseph J., ... 49 Manhattan Avenue, Brooklyn
Low, C. Adolph, ... : 41 Liberty Street, New York City
Low, Seth, ... 30 E. 64th Street, " " "
Low, William G., ... 58 Remsen Street, Brooklyn
Low, William, G. Jr., ... 58 Remsen Street, "
Lowell, Thomas W., ... 28 S. Portland Avenue, "
Lowndes, James, . . . 1505 Pennsylvania Avenue, Washington, D. C.
Luther, George Martin, ... 32 Liberty Street, New York City
Lyman, George T., ... Bellport, N. Y.
Lyman, Frank, ... 50 Remsen Street, Brooklyn
Lynde, Rollin H., . . ' ' ' 31 Pine Street, New York City

Macdonough, A. R., ... P. O. Box 839, New York City
Macfarlane, Wallace, ... 32 Liberty Street, " " "
MacVeagh, Charles, ... 17 Broad Street, " " "
Magee, John H., ... Scottsburg, N. Y.
Mallinckrodt, Edward, . Mallinckrodt Chemical Works, St. Louis, Mo.
Mapes, Charles V., ... 143 Liberty Street, New York City
Marquand, Henry, ... 160 Broadway, " " "
Marquand, Henry G., ... 11 E. 68th Street, " " "
Marshall, Charles H., ... 7 Nassau Street, " " "
Marshall, Fielding L., ... 55 Liberty Street, " " "
Martin, Newell, ... 7 Nassau Street, " " "
Martin, T. Comerford, . . . 120 Liberty Street, " " "
Mason, Alfred Bishop, ... Apartado 130, City of Mexico
Mason, James Weir, ... 32 W. 129th Street, New York City
Matthews, Robert, ... 96 Spring Street, Rochester, N. Y.
Matthewson, Arthur, ... 139 Montague Street, Brooklyn
Maxwell, Henry W., ... 70 First Place, "
Maxwell, William H., ... 682 Greene Avenue, "
Mellen, Chase, ... 45 Cedar Street, New York City

Merrill, Charles E.,   .   . . 48 E. 10th Street, New York City
Merrill, Payson, ... 111 Broadway, " " "
Miller, Jacob F., ... 120 Broadway, " " "
Mitchell, Edward, ... 31 E. 50th Street, " " "
Moffat,, George B.,   . . . 1 Nassau Street, " " "
Moffat, R. Burnham, ... 63 Wall Street, " " "
Montgomery, R. M., ... 61 Pine Street, " " "
Moore, J. H., ... 423 Madison Avenue, " " "
Moore, W. H. H., ... Box 402, " " "
Morse, James H., ... 423 Madison Avenue, " " "
Morse, Richard, C., ... 139 E.. 18th Street, " " "
Mortimer, Richard, ... 11 Wall Street, " " "
Mosenthal, P. J., ... 46 Cedar Street, " " "
Mott, William H., ... Toms River, N. J.
Munro, J. G., ... 19 South Division Street, Buffalo
Murray, James B., ... 69 Wall Street, New York City
Murray, Joseph K., ... 63 Wall Street, " " "
McAlpin, George L.,   . . . 9 E. 90th Street, New York City
McAneny, George, ... City Club " " "
McCagg, Louis Butler, .   . . 291 Madison Avenue, " " "
McCullough, Hall Park,   . . . 15 Broad Street, " " "
McKeen, James, ... 136 Henry Street, Brooklyn
McKeever, J. Lawrence,   . . 164 Lexington Avenue, New York City
McKelvey, John Jay,   . . . 66 Broadway, " " "
McKibben, Gilbert H.,   . . . 474 W. Broadway, " " "
McMahon, Fulton, ... 111 Broadway, " " "

Nadal, Charles C.,   . . . 129 E. 17th Street, New York City
Naumberg, Elkan, ... 6 Wall Street, " " "
Nelson, Henry Loomis,   . . . Harper & Bros., " " "
Nelson, H. W., Jr., ... Geneva, N. Y.
Nevius, John H. C.,   . . . 420 Broome Street, New York City
Newton, Virginius, ... Box 906, Richmond, Va.
Nichols, George M., ... 277 Adelphi St., Brooklyn
Nichols, W. N., ... 353 Clinton Avenue, "
Nicoll, James C., ... 51 W. 10th Street, New York City
North, Thomas M.,   . . 160 Central Park South, " " "

Ogden, Willis L., ... 73 Pierrepont Street, Brooklyn
Olin, Stephen H., ... 32 Nassau Street, New York City
Olyphant, Robert, .   . . 21 Cortlandt Street, " " "
Opdyke, William S.,   . . . 20 Nassau Street, " " "
Orr, Alexander E.,   . . . 102 Remsen Street, Brooklyn
Osborne, Thomas M., ... Auburn, N. Y.

Packard, Edwin, ... 241 Henry Street, Brooklyn
Parker, Frederick S.,   . . . 32 Garden Place, "
Parrish, Samuel L, ... 44 Broadway, New York City
Parsons, Herbert, ... 111 Broadway, " " "
Parsons, John E., ... 111 Broadway, " " "
Paulding, James Kirk,   . . 146 Forsyth Street, " " "

Pauli, H. G., ... 15 S. William Street, New York City
Peabody, George Foster, ... 27 Pine Street, " " "
Peck, George G., ... 18 East 65th Street, " " "
Pendleton, Franois K., ... 44 Broadway, " " "
Perrine, William A., ... 91 Centre Street, " " "
Phillips, Lee, ... 247 W. 71st Street, " " "
Phoenix, Phillips, ... 28 State Street, " " "
Pierce, Franklin, ... 120 Broadway, " " "
Pierrepont, Henry E., ... 216 Columbia Heights, Brooklyn
Pierrepont, H. E., Jr., ... 216 Columbia Heights, "
Pinchot, Gifford, ... 2 Gramercy Park, New York City
Pope, A. A., ... Pope Building, Boston
Pope, George A., ... P. O. Box 53, Baltimore, Md.
Pott, James, . . . Fourth Ave. and 22d Street, New York City
Potter, Frederick, ... Potter Bldg., " " "
Potter, Henry C., . . 10 Washington Square, East, " " "
Potts, William, ... 229 Lexington Avenue, " " "
Prentice, William P., ... 155 Broadway, " " "
Prentiss, George L., ... 41 E. 61st Street, " " "
Pryer, Charles, ... New Rochelle, N. Y.
Putnam, George Haven, ... 27 W. 23d Street, New York City
Putnam, Harrington, ... 404 Washington Avenue, Brooklyn
Putnam, Irving, ... 27 W. 23rd Street, New York City
Pyne, Moses Taylor, ... 42 W. 53d Street, " " "

Rand, George C., ... 107 Wall Street, New York City
Raymond, Charles H., ... 32 Liberty Street, " " "
Raymond, Rossiter W. . . . , . 123 Henry Street, Brooklyn
Reynolds, James B., ... 184 Eldridge Street, New York City
Rice, Edwin T., Jr., , ...59 Wall Street, " " "
Richards, C. A. L., ... 144 Benefit Street, Providence, R. I.
Richards, George, ... 62 Wall Street, New York City
Ritchie, John, ... 10 Mount Vernon Street, Boston
Rives, George L., ... 14 W. 38th Street. New York City
Robb, J. Hampden, ... 23 Park Avenue, " " "
Rogers, Henry A. . . . . . 19 John Street, " " "
Romaine, Benjamin F., Jr., . . . 20 Nassau Street, " " "
Romaine, Louis Tyson, ... 84 Beaver Street, " " "
Roome, W. Harris, ... 40 Wall Street, " " "
Roosevelt, Theodore, ... Executive Mansion, Albany, N. Y.
Root, Elihu, ... 32 Liberty Street, New York City
Ropes, John C., ... 99 Mt. Vernon Street, Boston
Rose, Arthur P., ... Geneva. N. Y.
Rosenblatt, M. G., (Life), . . . 35 Mercer Street, New York City
Rowe, William V., ... 52 Wall Street, " " "
Rumsey, Dexter P., ... 742 Delaware Street, Buffalo, N. Y.
Russell, Charles H., ... 15 Broad Street, New York City

Saint Gaudens, Augustus, ... 3 Rue de Bagneux, Paris
Salomon, William, ... 30 Broad Street, New York City

Sand, Max E., , ...	31 Burling Slip, New York City
Sands, B. Aymar, ...	31 Nassau Street " " "
Sands, Phillip J., ...	15 E. 33d Street, " " "
Sanger, William Cary, ...	Sangerfield, N. Y.
Sayer, W. Murray, Jr., . . .	398 Washington Avenue, Brooklyn
Schieren, Charles A. . . .	405 Clinton Avenue, "
Schumacher, Charles, . .	50 Exchange Place, New York City
Schurman, Jacob Gould, . . .	Cornell University, Ithaca, N. Y.
Schurz, Carl, ...	16 E. 64 Street, New York City
Schurz, Herbert.	16 E. 64 Street, " " "
Schwab, Henry C., . . .	2 Bowling Green, " " "
Scott, J. F., . . . , .	407 W. 123d Street, " " "
Scribner, Arthur H., . .	153 Fifth Avenue, " " "
Scribner, Charles, . .	153 Fifth Avenue, " " "
Searle, Arthur, . . .	41 Concord Avenue, Cambridge, Mass.
Seaver, Benjamin F., . . .	111 Pierrepont Street, Brooklyn
Sedgwick, Arthur G., . . .	115 Broadway. New York City
Seligman, E. R. A., . . ' .	324 W. 86th Street, " " "
Serven, A. Ralph, . .	Civil Service Commission, Washington, D. C.
Sexton, Lawrence E., ...	34 Pine Street, New York City
Shaw, Albert, , . . .	13 Astor Place, " " "
Shearman, Thomas G., . . .	176 Columbia Heights, Brooklyn
Shepard, Edward M., ...	111 Broadway, New York City
Shillaber, William A. Jr., ...	1 Broadway, " " "
Simes, William, ...	, Petersham, Mass.
Sinclair, John, . . .	521 Madison Avenue, New York City
Slicer, Thomas R., . . .	27 W. 76th Street, " " "
Slosson, Henry L., ...	Geneva, N. Y.
Slosson, J. Lawrence, ...	" "
Smillie, James D., ...	110 E. 38th Street, New York City
Smith, Charles Robinson, . . .	7 Nassau Street, " " "
Smith, Charles Stewart, . . .	20 E. 23d Street, " " "
Smith, Clarence B., ...	45 Broadway, " " "
Smith, J. Henry, . . .	10 Wall Street, " " "
Smith, William Alexander, . . .	70 Broadway, " " "
Snow, Henry Sanger, ...	81 Willoughby Street, Brooklyn
Stapler, H. B. B., ...	67 Wall Street, New York City
Stark, Joshua, ...	Milwaukee, Wis.
Stedman, Edmund C., . . .	16 Broad Street, New York City
Steers, James R., ...	55 Liberty Street, " " "
Stewardson, Thomas, . .	Chestnut Hill, Philadelphia, Pa.
Stickney, Joseph, ...	P. O. Box 2379, New York City
Stimson, Daniel M., . . .	11 W. 17th Street, " " "
Stoiber, Louis, . . , .	722 Broadway, " " "
Stokes, Anson Phelps, Jr., (Life), .	229 Madison Avenue,, " " "
Stokes, Harold M. Phelps, (Life), .	229 Madison Avenue, " " "
Stokes, I. N. Phelps, (Life), ' .	229 Madison Avenue, " " "
Stokes, James, . . . , .	49 Cedar Street, " " "
Stokes, J. G. Phelps, (Life), .	229 Madison Avenue, " " "

Straus, Frederick,	. 15 Broad Street, New York City
Storrs Richard S.,	. 80 Pierrepont Street, Brooklyn
Straus, Albert,	. 15 Broad Street, New York City
Stuart, William C.,	. . . . Pasadena, California
Sturges, S. Perry,	305 Washington Avenue, Brooklyn
Sturgis, Russell, .	307 E. 17th Street, New York City
Sturgis, Thomas, .	. 138 E. 36th Street, " " "
Stuyvesant, Rutherford,	16 Exchange Place, " " "
Swan, Lyndon M.,	. 31 Pine Street, " " "
Taber, John R., .	. 714 Water Street, New York City
Tatham, Charles, .	302 Lexington Avenue, " " "
Tatham, Edwin, . .	. 82 Beekman Street, " " "
Taylor, Thomas Fenton,	. . 31 Nassau Street, " " "
Taylor, William C., .	. . . . 94 Keap Street, Brooklyn
Terry, Roderick,	. 169 Madison Avenue, New York City
Terry, Seth Sprague,	. . 66 Broadway, " " "
Thompson, Hugh S.,	. . 346 Broadway, " " "
Thomson, William H.,	. 23 E. 47th Street, " " "
Thurber, Francis B.,	. 143 Chambers Street, " " "
Tiebout. Charles H.,	. . . 31 Grand Street, Brooklyn
Tod, J. Kennedy, .	. . 45 Wall Street, New York City
Tomkins, Calvin,	. 32 Liberty Street, " " "
Tompkins, Hamilton B.,	. . 229 Broadway, " " "
Trenholm, W. L., .	. . 160 Broadway, " " "
Turnbull, George R., .	. . . 33 Mercer Street, " " "
Turner, Herbert B.,	. . 22 William Street, " " "
Tweedy, Edmund,	. 25 Bellevue Court, Newport, R. I.
Valentine, Henry C., (Life),	. . 57 Broadway, New York City
Vallandingham, Edward N.,	. . Reform Club, " " "
Vanderpoel, John,	36 W. 39th Street, " " "
Van Dusen, Samuel C.,	. . 39 Cliff Street, " " "
Van Iderstine, Robert,	. 20 Nassau Street, " " "
Van Ingen, Dudley W.,	. . . 135 Henry Street, Brooklyn
Van Ingen, Edward H.,	. . 9 E. 71st Street, New York City
Van Nest, George W.,	. .. 32 Nassau Street, " " "
Van Sinderen, Howard,	. . 15 Broad Street, " " "
Villard, Henry, (Life), . . ,	145 W. 58th Street, " " "
Villard, Oswald Garrison, .	. . . 206 Broadway, " " "
Wadsworth, James W.,	. . . . Geneseo, N. Y.
Walker, Hay, . . .	. Care of W. & H. Walker, Alleghany City, Pa.
Walker, John, . .	. Care of W. & H. Walker, " "
Walker, Samuel C.,	. . . Harbison & Walker, Pittsburg, Pa.
Walker, William, .	. Care of W. & H. Walker, Allegheny City, Pa.
Wallace, Jackson,	. . .32 Liberty Street, New York City
Wallace, William H.,	. . . . 66 Broadway, " " "

Ward, Henry Galbreath,	. 160 Broadway, New York City
Ward, J. H.,	. 19 Kenyon Bldg., Louisville, Ky.
Ward, J. Q. A.,	. 119 W. 52nd Street, New York City
Ward, S. G.,	. 15 Broad Street, " " "
Warner, John De Witt,	. 111 Broadway, " " "
Warren, E. Walpole,	823 Madison Avenue, " " "
Warren, George A.,	620 I Street, N. W., Washington, D. C.
Warren, H. Langford,	. 9 Park Street, Boston, Mass.
Webb, William H.,	. 415 Fifth Avenue, New York City
Weed, John W.,	. 62 William Street, " " "
Weeks, E. R.,	503 Delaware Street, Kansas City, Mo.
Weeks, Rufus W.,	. 348 Broadway, New York City
Wehle, Theodore,	32 Liberty Street, " " "
Welling, R. W. G.,	. 2 Wall Street, " " "
Weston, Edward,	P. O. Box 617, Yonkers, N. Y.
Weston, Walter,	584 North Broadway, " "
Wheeler, A. S.,	, 511 Sears Bldg., Boston, Mass.
Wheeler, Everett P.,	. 45 Broadway, New York City
Wheeler, James R.,	. Columbia College, " " "
White, Alexander M.,	. 2 Pierrepont Place, Brooklyn
White, Alexander M., Jr.,	158 Columbia Heights, "
White, Andrew D., (Life),	American Embassy, Berlin
White, George C.,	. P. O. Box 320, New York City
White, Horace,	. 18 W. 69th Street, " " "
White, William Augustus,	. 130 Water Street, " " "
Whitehead, Charles E.,	. 71 Wall Street, " " "
Whitlock, Bache McE.,	. 49 Wall Street, " " "
Whitridge, Frederick W.,	. 59 Wall treet, " " "
Wickersham, George W.,	. 40 Wall Street, " " "
Wiggin, Frederick H.,	. 55 W. 36th Street, " " "
Wilcox, Ansley,	. 298 Main Street, Buffalo, N. Y.
Wilcox, David,	Metropolitan Club, New York City
Williams, L. L.,	. 316 W. 78th Street, " " "
Wilson, Richard T.,	. 511 Fifth Avenue, " " "
Wing, Henry T.,	. 152 Clinton Street, Brooklyn
Winslow, Edward,	. P. O. Box 486, New York City
Wise, B. E.,	21 Broad Street, New York City
Wisner, Charles,	. Cotton Exchange, " " "
Wisner, H. G.,	. 18 W. 12th Street, " " "
Wolff, Louis S.,	. 12 E. 70th Street, " " "
Wood, Walter R.,	. 17 Broadway, " " "
Woodbridge, Charles E.,	. 44 Pine Street, " " "
Wright, Jonathan,	73 Remsen Street, Brooklyn
Yonge, Henry,	Hotel Margaret, Brooklyn
York, John C.,	. Huntington, L I.
Young, J. A.,	. Warrensburg, Mo.
Zabriskie, George,	. 17 Broad Street, New York City
Zerega, Richard A.,	. 38 W. 48th Street, " " "